YVETTE ESHIBA

Fired Before You're Hired

A Christian's survival guide for the secular workplace

This book was professionally typeset on Reedsy.
Find out more at reedsy.com

I dedicate my first born book to the Lord of Lords and King of Kings. His name is Yeshua Hamashiach . He is the one who gave me the experiences that will give people hope and comfort because their stories are unbelievable.

"Misunderstanding, is understanding to the person who misunderstood" - Myles Munroe

Contents

I

Part One

1

WHAT GIVES

P icture this; you attain your high school diploma. Check. You acquire your undergraduate degree after a grueling 5 years away from home. Check. You've completed several internships; surely one of them will hire you. Check. That first offer wasn't sufficient enough, so you keep looking for work. You land your first job in a fortune 500 company. Check. Congratulations! You took a job in a great company as a Secretary thinking they will see your credentials and potential and promote you to that wonderful job you've always wanted, but still didn't have enough experience and that 'foot in the door' got stuck - so you had to look elsewhere and take what you really want because you'll never be happy supporting other people doing what you've always wanted to do. You find yourself in similar situations in different places and you experience a lot of frustration. Then it gets worse. Once people find out that you are a devout, born again, spirit filled, believer in Christ - even without you saying a word - you become scum around the office. You become a target for torment. People find fault with you wherever they can, and suddenly, those who were pleasant acquaintances become enemies the first time you don't agree with their sinful shenanigans. The minute you come through the doors, people stop talking or engage in side conversations difficult for you to hear. You're wondering what's happening. You want to inquire, or defend yourself against the false accusations and persecution when you realize, this goes with the territory. You don't belong. You never will belong. You will never fit. And this, my friend, puts you in a lonely place. A place of scourging from your coworkers. A place of misunderstanding and betrayal. A place that makes you promotable to God because you were not willing to go along to get along where sin plays a role. You know you're not perfect, but all they see is the light exposing darkness. You then realize, you are not of this world. You have another citizenship they know not of, however, you are determined for them to know you in the most tactful, polite, loving, respectful way. You may be qualified for the job, but despised in the workplace. 'You're fired from our friendship (they may say)! But, we'll use what we can tolerate from you.' Don't take it personally; love the sinner anyway!

Citizenship in God's Kingdom

Welcome to God's kingdom. You probably never looked at it that way when you became a born again believer and follower of Christ, but, here we are. Invisible God, invisible kingdom, very powerful government with laws, power, and authority, embellished with blessings, unconditional love, and instructions on how to live your life. Throughout the years I've heard people frown at the thought of anyone telling them how to 'live their lives'. Christians have a whole manual. The more we read, understand, and practice, the more we see how real this invisible kingdom is. Colossians 1:16 states "For through him God created everything in the heavenly realms and on earth. He made the things we can see and the things we can't see— such as thrones, kingdoms, rulers, and authorities in the unseen world. Everything was created through him and for him." *(New Living Translation:Bible Hub, 2024)*. We can't afford to minimize Christianity. Heaven is our home. Earth is our mission to spread the gospel, and we are on assignment as Christ's Ambassadors. Christian will not be celebrated in every place. Once they discover what you believe, the rejection begins.

Another aspect we need to understand about our citizenship in God's Kingdom is that the world even understands the rules and have inevitably applied them in a portion of the world system: the court system, the school system *(at one time)*, and even some secret societies who swear they are living in and practicing kingdom principles. Let's look at it like this: there is a structure and a government that you represent now. You're official. You are a King and a Priest in this kingdom *(no gender recognized)*. You are a spirit, you have a soul, and you live in a physical body. You've been born again, blood washed, blood bought, redeemed from the curse of the law, and now you stand in a place where you are being prepared to even judge angels and ultimately fight in a battle called Armageddon. We won't go deeply into that now, but these are just a few things to name that God is qualifying you for. Colossians 1:13 tells us that God has translated us from darkness to the kingdom of the Son He loves *(New Living Translation:Bible Hub, 2024)*. Did you know what you were getting yourself into? Kingdom of light citizens have much ahead in life. The good news is, God has equipped you with everything you need; and He's going to send a few good men to groom you for your true purpose in His kingdom. Don't turn back - just keep moving forward. Work as if you are working for the Lord wherever you go, but keep your eyes open watchmen.

The most noticeable

The first thing I noticed in corporate America that would cause co-worker separation was the various stereotypes. Our society is hypocritical. They say not to judge a book by its cover, but they always do. If you are Black, you are thought to be ignorant, criminal, but on the other hand, athletic and talented. As an African American professional, I found many situations appalling. I'll never forget my first temporary job. I was typing a presentation in the marketing department of a fortune 500 company. The company was having a picnic on the grounds that day. A senior Caucasian man came to me and asked if I wanted to attend the picnic. As I expressed the urgency of the project I was working on, he told me they had good watermelon and chicken. I didn't reply with anything but a smile and a reserved "thank you", because I understood that he misunderstood. I couldn't get angry, because I understood that society was being reflected through a kind man who thought he was doing a great deed. Other stereotypes tend to bombard our society that I'm almost 99% sure you are aware of; which leads me to my next observation.

Isms

Jocelyn Elders, contributor to the definition "ISM" in Webster's dictionary, views its meaning as "an oppressive and especially discriminatory attitude or belief "we all have got to come to grips with our ism". The terrible truth is, whether we want to admit it or not, there's a little 'ism' in all of us. We all just haven't come to ism realities when we bring it into our families, our relationships, our choices and moreover, our workplaces. Frankly, anyone who hasn't experienced practicing or being a victim of an "ism" just doesn't exist on this planet. As a high school teacher, in a Journalism class I've taught, this was one of the most interesting class lessons. Function in the private corporation, as well as the public school system and the church, I understand what is meant to be politically correct, however, my students and I threw those rules out of the window, I drew a cage on the board, and asked the class the name "isms" they'd heard of. Racism, sexism, classism, levelism, ageism, and of course some smarty pants would name an ism that I couldn't go into in terms of applying the meaning to today's society (*i.e., fascism, communism, sectarianism, etc)*. While we know racism discriminates against one's race or culture, sexism is when people make a difference between men and women. In America, a man and woman can have the same job and the woman gets paid less. A man and woman can live in the same household and have various domestic jobs to do. Throwing out garbage and repairing the house is for the 'man', while washing dishes and clothes, cooking and cleaning windows is for the 'woman'. How absurd. I do understand that the sexes have different chemistry, motivation, and interests, many don't have the luxury, for example, single parent families, single or disabled citizens, homes where children or spouses have been abandoned for some reason or another. One's determination 'kicks' in and they do whatever is necessary to get the job done. Even I have had co-teachers who thought, because of their credentials, they didn't have to do the small, but necessary things in the classroom to help the main teacher. What they didn't know, was that I shared some of the same, if not more credentials; and understood that all jobs, small or great, required my attention and interaction, so that students had what they needed, even to the point of their grades being received sooner than later so they'd have time to redo or correct their error. Do whatever it takes, when you're professional, mature, qualified, wise, and understanding of your job. It makes you promotable, efficient, marketable, desirable by employers and smarter. Don't get caught up in the 'isms' that "this is your job, this is my job, and I don't do that". It shows you don't understand the big picture. Don't get me wrong, don't abuse yourself or be abused. Sometimes you have to say no to the person who is still functioning in the 'ism' standard. You must set necessary boundaries so you're not abused, mistreated or misused. But be the one that they watch and say "now that's a competent, dependable, employee – give him/her the promotion".

Sometimes we are challenged in our jobs to engage in 'isms'. I remember working as an intern journalist for an African American city newspaper. We received a call in the newsroom about a bus driver who beat up a passenger. It so happened the bus driver was a Caucasian male, while the passenger he assaulted was an African American female. You should have seen the thoughts going through my head of how to structure the story. Is it that a man attacked a woman? A professional attacked a client? A White attacked a Black? Or a White male attacked a Black female? I stuck to the professional attacking a client who just happened to be, etc. It takes me back to Hurricane Katrina, which yielded news reports of Caucasians taking food for survival and African Americans taking food as 'looting.'

Christians, I know you're wondering, how does this apply to me? I'll tell you how, you are part of the 'ism' in our modern day society. You will be discriminated against because of your beliefs.

Discrimination

The Berean Study Bible says in Matthew 10:22 "You will be hated by everyone on account of My name, but the one who perseveres to the end will be saved." Face it, Saints. A secular artist, Teddy Pendergrass, put the concept so plainly in his lyrics that is so applicable to us. "You can't hide from yourself, everywhere you go, there you are." You need to understand what goes with the package of being born again; being born of God and being true, devout Christian. There are so many things that occur in the secular and, I might add, Christian workplace, that go against the ways of God. As a professional, I understand that we must be flexible and somewhat tolerant to be effective. It's important to know that everyone is not a Christian, and shouldn't be expected to behave like one . . . better yet, talk the language that Christians talk. While we are to have Christian standards to live by, we must not forget our 24 hour, 365 days a year, daily duty toward our heavenly father according to the book Ecclesiastes 12:13. The New American Standard Bible states "The conclusion, when all has been heard, is: fear God and keep His commandments, because this applies to every person." Think of how Jesus changed the 10 commandments and condensed them to 2 new ones. Matthew 22: 35-40 35 And one of them, a lawyer, asked him a question, trying him:

36 Teacher, which is the great commandment in the law? 37 And he said unto him, Thou shalt <u>love the Lord thy God with all thy heart, and with all thy soul, and with all thy mind</u>. 38 This is the great and first commandment. 39 And a second like [unto it] is this, Thou shalt <u>love thy neighbor as thyself</u>. 40 On these two commandments the whole law hangeth, and the prophets.

This is so ingenious of Jesus to change things. No, not change; simplify. Truth is, Love covers everything. You will face discrimination in the workplace. Just don't give place to the devil in your attitude. Understand that some are in bondage to see people the way the enemy has manipulated them. Know that God is on your side, and He's more than the world against you.

Many philosophers have ideas on the duties of 'mankind' so-to-speak. A famous 17th century German Philosopher, Samuel Pufendorf, originated the writing and observation of several accounts concerning the whole duty of man according to the law of nature. What I believe Pufendorf may have overlooked, is that spiritual laws should influence natural laws where born again believers are concerned. A true believer's actions should be a manifestation of his spiritual maturity and mandate. *(Wrenn, 2016)*

Character cookie cutter syndrome

I've always been different. I wasn't trying; it just happened. Saved and on fire for God as a youth made a difference in my character. I couldn't get away with doing what everybody else was. I couldn't live with myself to think the way society expected me to think. When I started working in corporate America, I realized that people were expected to be carbon copies instead of originals. While I believe that originals ultimately become distinguished leaders and possess leadership qualities from it, there's not much room in the world for originality unless it's in the form of some type of entertaining talent. You dress the same, walk the same, talk the same, eat the same, handle problems the same: it's a culture. I've also discovered that if you didn't fit into the corporate culture; one way, or another, you would be out of there. Either by being driven, or fired for no legitimate reason. I've been fired from a couple corporate jobs where in the exit interview my question of "what is the real reason I'm getting fired" was always answered with a vague "you're not producing up to the level of expectation." What I couldn't understand was, if it was an entry-level job, I was already overqualified. Even to the point of getting compliments from clients on my way out the door. Oh, let's not forget the firing for making my department *(of 10)* feel 'uncomfortable', even after turning in a 10 page- report on all the harassment I was experiencing, to human resources, who by the way, made an excuse for everything except the sexual one. They were willing to pursue the offending co-worker if I wanted. I imagined maybe they wanted that guy out of there, so they didn't mind supporting me with that particular incident.

You really can't always express your views and opinions in a secular workplace. Think about it. You spend more time at work with coworkers than sometimes at home with family. If you don't count sleeping hours. I've seen young believers in Christ make the mistake of being overzealous in their workplaces, often resulting in them getting fired. That is the result of a lack of maturity and knowledge. As God's children grow in His grace, their eyes are opened to Paul's suggestion to ".... those without the Law I became like one without the Law *(though I am not outside the law of God but am under the law of Christ)*, to win those without the Law. To the weak I became weak, to win the weak. I have become all things to all men so that by all possible means I might save some of them. 23:I do all this for the sake of the gospel, so that I may share in its blessings...." I Corinthians 9:21-23 *(KJV, Bible Hub, 2024)*

You can't hide

We must realize that when we are in Christ, and we are filled with His Spirit and His fire, we're going to burn everywhere we go; even without saying a word. The Bible tells us that darkness hates light, "Everyone who does evil hates the light, and will not come into the light for fear that their deeds will be exposed" *(KJV: Biblehub. John 3:20).* To put it plainly, most of my personal experience of opposition and attack came from people who support the homosexual agenda or, as some preachers say, 'the Alphabet people'. Without saying one word about Jesus' advocacy for heterosexual lifestyle, I was constantly attacked, rejected, and rebutted without saying one word. People would defend the darkness that my light exposed. There is a Christian saying to 'Preach the gospel, and if necessary, use words." How true it is. Our lives are like an open book that people will read. They may not like what they see, but it's our lives, hidden in Christ. Except we end up being a light to a whole dark world whose minds have been blinded, whose sins have them in captivity, who, when their eyes are opened, may cry out to the Lord for help. Just be there. Be the salt and light you were destined to be. When persecution and tough times come in the workplace, know that it is inevitable. It is bound to happen. And like I tell some of my students, "suck it up cupcake", because it's going to make you strong in the Lord, when you are handling it God's way.

2

CORPORATE AMERICA

Personality clashes
Someone who mattered once said 'No two people are alike'. I agree. We may look alike, dress alike, speak the same language, have similar interests, but we must face the reality that people are still distinguished by some personality trait(s). So what if you're raised in a totally different culture from your coworkers, have different practices or opinions about life. See people and the world in a different light. One corporate giant maintained a theme that claimed "the world is shaped by diversity". It was a reference to acceptance of alternative lifestyles in the workplace as the generational mindsets changed and sexual preferences became more like an exposé. However, I took it literally. While people were throwing machetes at the devoutness of my Christian lifestyle, I threw back in their faces that I was among the diverse and have a right to be just as much tolerated and accepted as any others with differences. Those glasses were one sided however. Like having a mirrored lens, on the inside; all one sees is himself in a world that doesn't revolve around him. Except he or she doesn't realize it doesn't revolve. Be yourself Christ-like believers. You have just as much right to have an opinion, take a stand *(short for standard)*, practice what

you preach, never compromise but always be flexible. Love God, yourself, and others. More importantly, don't let the looks, comments, stares, whispers, and actions wound you. As God told Prophet Jeremiah "Get up and prepare for action. Go out and tell them everything I tell you to say. Do not be afraid of them, or I will make you look foolish in front of them." Don't make the mistake of being self-righteous. Your righteousness is nothing; only the righteousness of God is everything. It will cause you to love your enemies and do the complete opposite of what the world expects.

Christianity clashes

When I encountered much in corporate America, there was nothing worse than not being able to locate another devout Christian. These days, vile, profane, drunken, whore mongering, idol worshiping, criminal, hypocrite, and just plain old Sunday and holiday churchgoers won't hesitate to raise their hand and say 'I'm a Christian'. Now don't get me wrong; Christianity is not founded on works, it just works on your foundation. Christians have sinned, will sin, and are sinning now; as you read. But, devout brothers and sisters don't practice sin, and if they sin, they have the blood of Jesus to cleanse them. Devout Christians really don't want to sin. It breaks God's heart, hurts themselves and others, and basically gives place to the devil. The Bible tells us that men will know we are Christians by the love we have one to another. There are many cold-hearted people in the house of God who have allowed their hurts to contaminate the God gifts inside them. Some have become bitter, resentful, and unforgiving; neither being able to give or receive love, nor help their brothers and sisters in the family *(body of Christ)*. So, it's like calling all saint's like people call the cops when there's an emergency and hearing an echo of their own voice. Better yet, they hear crickets chirping because Christians are not standing their ground in the workplace. We need more unity in the body of Christ. We must break

13

down these denominational barriers, racial barriers *(yes, there is still racism and other isms in the church)*, and get rid of the pride or shame in our lives. The end times are especially a time to be that friend that sticks closer than a brother. Jesus led this by example, and so can you. I haven't seen strong, loving, accountable, godly workplace relationships in a while and learned to live without it-if I have minimal or no choice; but it's a refreshing oasis when it comes.

Corporate culture

The corporate world has its own standards. It's like corporate America is its own planet. It has its own atmosphere, way to dress, way to talk, walk, look, shake hands, use politics, communicate, and relate to others. Eight out of 10 times, brothers and sisters, you've got to learn it to earn it; that is, respect in this world. The work ethic, while beneficial to many, is sometimes the opposite of true Christianity. Some may disagree with what is about to be said, however, this is my observation and experience of 12 years there. The following are just a few things Christians SHOULD be doing: adhering to company rules, being at work on time *(even early)*, dressing professionally, articulating words, being an effective communicator, be educated or still pursuing education, smiling and speaking to people (no matter how you feel), fulfilling your tasks and then some, attending some social corporate events (dinners, trade shows, retirement parties, social events at conferences and retreats, etc.) showing your boss and coworkers diversity, dependability, commitment, and trustworthiness and finally, maturity. Demonstrate good character and integrity as a habit. The following are just a few things Christians should NOT be doing: coming late and reporting you're on time, dressing the way you want and not in adherence to the company standard, using foul or perverted language to entertain or relate to coworkers, working hard only when the boss is looking, displaying a sad countenance all the time, becoming withdrawn *(hey! You can smile and nod and be a good listener without compromising your values.)* We are IN the world, but not OF the world. Remember, Jesus was always around publicans and sinners. He said "it's not the well who need a doctor, but those who are sick." How will our lights shine if we hide it under a bush? Christians should not steal from the company; this includes materials, time, money. Don't get drunk at corporate events, and really, try to avoid saying or laughing at dirty jokes. A proverbial saying in Galatians 5:9 states "A little yeast works through the whole batch of dough." You want to stay as pure and unspotted as God has provided you the tools to do so. It's like putting one drop of food coloring in a cup of water. The water is no longer pure, it's colored, and you'd need a whole new cup to start over. Some of us need to recommit our lives to Christ because we've become so conformed to the world, not transformed with a renewed mind. *(NIV. Bible. Bible Hub, 2024)*

Temporary agencies vs permanent employment

When it comes to integrity, and values, it just doesn't matter if you're working for a week, a month, or a year; be consistent in your character at all times. A temporary job is just as important as a permanent position, if not more, because you must make a positive impression quickly. Not too much time to impress, and you don't have a 2nd time to make a first impression. Right away, a new employer or new potential employer who took a risk to have you on board, hopes they made the right decision. Don't go on a new job, or better yet, any job, not doing your best. You are representing Christ and are to work as if for Him and not just an individual. You also don't do your best only when the boss is looking. *(Ephesians 6:5-9)* By the way, for you neophytes, companies monitor your every move even more these days than ever before. They monitor your phone calls and conversations, they monitor your internet usage and your various usage of the computer. They have cameras in the areas you work – even in the bathrooms. If, however, you find one in a stall, it could be a lawsuit; however, you have to prove it, and cameras can be the size of a pinhead, so you'll have to do your research. I'm telling you this because I've learned from my own mistakes of excessive use of the internet when I had dead-end jobs that just didn't challenge me; even jobs where I've had 2 hours worth of work on an 8-hour shift. Or maybe I tried to edit a manuscript brought to work from my home based business or tried to use company tools to create a project like a family calendar. I got in so much trouble for that, but it was covert, subtle, intentional, indirect, and sometimes illegal. Problem is. . . . my coworkers got away with everything. I knew that God wasn't allowing me to do things that didn't honor Him too long, so I discontinued those things. Yes, I learned the hard way. Just so you know, for Christians, the Bible says God's judgment comes first to us.(*I Peter 4:17*) Whom the Lord loves, He chastises. (*Hebrews 12:6*) Your conscience is governed by the Holy Spirit, and He will show you all things. Nothing like a spiritual spanking in your consciousness. God helps His children represent Him well, so endeavor to do good at all times. Even if man doesn't give you a second chance; God will.

Remote triggers

One of the luxuries of remote jobs is that we don't have the office drama to contend with. In my 2nd career as Secondary Educator, this luxury is even more fulfilling. Every time I tell someone my profession, they cringe and say "you're a good one," "I could never do that," "God bless your ministry." After 2 decades I can't imagine teaching without knowing God. It feels nearly impossible now - however, I know better: 'All things are possible to those who believe'. The stress of being a teacher in an impoverished community my entire career has created more compassion in my heart while simultaneously yielded a lot of frustration from the mental stress, and as I age, the physical challenges. But enough about me, let's open our eyes and look at the screen. One of the most challenging times of my life that became a spiritual war was when I got attacked online. This occurred in my early 30s. I'll tell you more about that story later in the book. As a teacher, my current profession, I experienced bullying and from an administrator known for haranguing his staff and student body when provoked. I noticed when we were on a call in a remote meeting, after he addressed us, the call was finished and people were slowly getting off line. He used spontaneous, aggressive profanity, but under his breath for whomever he was addressing. It sounded like a threat. I almost took it personally because I connected it to his offensive behavior in the workplace when no one else was looking except me. People tend to get angry because they can't control you. They can't make you fear them or make you lose your joy. There are all kinds of ways people can insult those they don't prefer. Sarcasm, euphemisms, gossip, slander, or making you the butt end of a bad joke. The Bible refers to it as coarse jesting. We're not to engage in it, but it doesn't stop the people walking in darkness.

3

EXPECT RETALIATION FOR DIFFERENCES

Silent snake

Don't be deceived, as the old southerners used to say, 'every goodbye ain't gone, every eye closed ain't sleep,' and as I say, 'every smile ain't happy'. You've all kinds of 'snakes' in the corporate world and none of them want to walk away without seizing their prey. Christians, young adults, are like sitting ducks. People have demons in them, around them, and they are not aware of what's working in them. I've lost several jobs once people *(employers, administrators)* discovered I was a devout Christian. I've had things done to me that you could not believe, because I didn't fit in. It was then that I realized there is no such thing as job security, but only, God security. I also did get a little discouraged about my degree and deemed it useless because of the vindictive things I would deal with to survive in the corporate world and in life in general.

Covert hate crimes

For example, if someone didn't like me, I'd get scratched hard on the back when they walked by, sexually harassed, my emails hacked, I've experienced workplace mobbing: a mob of Indian tech guys loudly come by my department while I worked nights alone, consultants and/or tech crew members making indiscriminate sounds on the intercom, again, while working nights alone, employees conversing with other employees right next to me, my actions of the day before arriving at work and what my bedroom looks like. I've been kicked *(or whatever you might call it when someone puts the bottom of their shoe on you and pushes himself off with his rolling chair)*; I've been watched closely as if a criminal and overtly mistreated. Some of these things happened after a conversation with another employee about my testimony, while actively doing my job, after I spent down time on Christian Debate *(on the internet)*, or my lunch time praying alone in the bathroom for a few minutes. It's amazing how people who hate you for your beliefs, have to attack you subtly and covertly in the workplace. I'll forgive, but I'll never forget these things.

Co-worker and employee persecution

Jamaicans use Obeah, Haitians and Trinidadians use voodoo, Cubans practice Santeria, Brazilians use Macumba, Africans, Juju, and the list goes on. You work with all kinds from various cultures and geographic locations where these things are practiced on a regular basis and may run in the family bloodlines of many. Don't think for one second that people don't or won't use witchcraft in the workplace. One thing I've learned to do is to connect the dots between the spiritual and natural. For example, I don't take for granted a 'black balling' *(everywhere you try to start new, negative references prevent you from getting anything, job, house, relationship)*. I discovered this when the majority of people were at lunch *(or meeting about me)*, I sent an email and heard the alarm immediately go off on a coworker's computer. I sent another email and the alarm went off again. I then sent an email to myself and the alarm went off again. coworkers in my department were given access to my email illegally and unethically, and thus, they manipulated my

19

communication and monopolized any plans or activities I would make. I then started preaching the gospel and sending the email to myself and they were all getting it, rolling their eyes, and complaining. They were having individual meetings with higher-ups and telling them they were uncomfortable to work around me. I say this because I overheard. This particular company was also the company where I experienced my first witchcraft headache. The sole-proprietor 'Mickey' used to come by and look in the glass window where we worked as if he were surprised to see I was still there. It was like, I disturbed the atmosphere, the people turned against me, and, because there was no legitimate reason to fire me, they actually were trying to drive me out with witchcraft. Because I didn't have a solid prayer life at that time.

If you study the life of Paul, you'll see his life was worse. I'm no comparison to Paul and all the beatings and imprisonment he encountered; getting attacked by mobs of people, shipwrecked, shedding blood; but Apostle Paul and I could relate to the persecution complex.

4

SECRET SOCIETY

hy I never pledged Greek
I didn't join because there was something about these organizations that didn't fit me. Something in my spirit would not mix, click or connect, and I had no control of it. Don't get me wrong, I wanted to pledge so badly I could taste it. Had offers, invitations to rush parties, applications handed to me, knew what I wanted to pledge, but it's like, when I was about to move forward, I stepped to an invisible glass door. I remember once stumbling upon a ritual for sweetheart pledgees. These are the female constituents who support the corresponding fraternities. They had been blindfolded, one took the wrong door, got out and one of the 'bros' had to quickly get her back into the room where the ritual was taking place. I thought 'that's odd, wonder what they're doing in there'. I've seen 'sweethearts' needing my help to 'cock block', that is, to prevent a sexual encounter with a fraternal member with whom they desperately avoided, because sex was part of the amenities of being a frat brother. If a frat brother knew she was a sweetheart to their organization, he could have sex with her, or better yet, any one of them. I came too late to be one, thank God, because, outside of a rape, I was a secondary virgin. I've seen girls crying because

they were mistreated by males in the fraternity they 'supported', and trying to pretend everything was ok because everything is confidential. Moreover, we all hear in the news about entire fraternity or sorority chapters getting kicked off campus for violence, extreme hazing, rape, and even murder. A college student told me of a pledgee from another campus who came to our campus who was hit by a sorority sister with a brick in a pillowcase;. Other stories included a line brother kicked in the groin so hard, he became infertile and sued a school. Still more, another pledgee died of a heart attack because they used a boom box that gave the sound effect of a train coming when they jokingly put him on the tracks tied up, blindfolded, and the list goes on. Hazing, it's called. Hell in motion, is what I call it. In the Washington CityPaper, Paul Ruffins, Reporter on June 18, 1999, records the story of a pledger who said "I began to have powerful feelings that I had to hurt myself to get away from these people," . . . He ultimately had to call a suicide hotline, resulting in his spending a week in George Washington University Hospital, being treated for depression and suicidal thoughts. Ruffins remarked that 'Pledging a Black frat can bring you status, connections, and lasting friendships. But an underground pledging process often includes paddling, assaults, and terror.

I kept asking myself, besides being a pretty and smart, party, college girl, what's the real reason I should be associated with this group. Then I asked a sorority sister who said "you do a lot of community service, and when you graduate from college, it's good networking. . . if your sorority sister is the boss, you get the job." I thought 'that's cool,' but I also thought, but the God I serve requires me to be a humanitarian by nature, and He Himself will open doors for me that no man can close. Flip the script for a minute; if a non-sorority sister is the boss, her kindred sorority sister will get priority over me no matter how qualified I am, and I don't like that. Bottom line, I understood there is a Greek god or goddess for every Greek organization to which you pledge. I don't know everything, but what I knew was enough. Even the word of God tells us in the book of James 5:12, "above all things, my brethren, swear not, neither by heaven, neither by earth, neither by any oath..." In a recent blog with Alton Jamison, initiator of a Christian Fraternity, he states "My argument is not that the pledging is bad, the colors or the organization itself, it's the oath that you say with your mouth, once you cross. You may say that it's a small thing. But life and death is in the power of the tongue. We are "snared" by the words of our mouth. When we take oaths, we are connecting ourselves to something other than our Lord and savior Jesus Christ. I am even against Christians saying "I swear to God" because the Bible says specifically "swear not". It just opens you up to ancient demons who are going to affect and infect you and your family bloodline, possibly getting you the money and possessions you want out of life, but possessing you, manipulating you, enslaving you, and victimizing you spiritually and naturally. Why give yourself more trouble – you're going to deal with enough trouble in life just because you're walking in the light. The following list Jamison writes as challenging questions to ask yourself whether you should or should not pledge a Greek organization:

1) Will you be required to take any oaths to anyone or anything outside of God (*Jesus Christ*)?

2) Will you be expected to support activities that you typically wouldn't support?

3) What activities does the organization do to win people to Christ?

4) Are you only in it for letters, or are you really going to work once you get in?

5) Will you feel "complete" once you get in or cross? If so, why?

6) Is it your dream or a relative's dream?

7) What would happen if you never join? Will you feel incomplete?

8) Do you have a problem partying at the dance and then teaching Bible study or going to church the next day?

9) Do you want people to first know you as a Christian or a part of an organization?

10) Did you really pray about it? And wait for an answer?

I know a brother who specifically took a stand after being a devout fraternity brother. After repenting of his sins and being born again, he renounced and denounced any affiliation, connection, relationship to the organization, burned the paraphernalia, stopped doing the call and the handshake, and was converted and renewed by Christ as he obeyed his spirit to totally walk away from it. He pastors a large church for more than 2 decades. On another hand, several other Christian students and I had an intense discussion as to whether or not we should pledge. We had mixed feelings, but several of us really wanted to, badly. We decided to all pray about it, and get this; if God told one of us 'yes', we were all going to pledge. If he told one of us 'no', none of us would pledge. How ironic and divine; God told us all 'no'. We obeyed. It was 'Me Phi Me' or 'G Phi G', but God was the only one we pledge our allegiance, life, love, and existence to. Never a better choice. Your creator, the one who made you, is the one who can fix you when you're broken, open doors for you that no man can close, make a way in the wilderness, turn your sorrow into joy and your mourning into dancing. God will give you wisdom beyond your years, can pull out of you witty and creative inventions, and make you a sign and a wonder to all mankind.

SSO's overall

What's wrong with some private organizations? Nothing, if you're a lover of divination, rankings, power and prestige with a sense of belongingness. Devout Christians who are knowledgeable about the kingdom of God should not have any part of it, however. The sin is in the secrecy. Many Christians are unaware until they actually join and get established in these organizations over a length of time. When Cain killed his brother Abel, he tried to hide it, deny it, and go on with his life - but he couldn't. There were negative consequences. He was protected by God, but condemned to be a vagabond. When Adam and Eve ate the forbidden fruit, they tried to hide it and move on with their lives, but they couldn't. They were cursed to work by the sweat of their brow; Eve suffered in childbirth, and they were kicked out of the garden of Eden - a great paradise. Ananias and Saphira kept back some money from the sales they made and said they gave the whole amount. As a result, they dropped dead for lying to the Holy Ghost, though they thought they were only talking to Peter. Usually when something is wrong, you try to hide it. Demons try to hide behind things. They will make it look appealing to you but it's full of hell. The Bible says Jesus spoiled and exposed principalities, to destroy the works of darkness. *(Colossians 2:15)* Christians, open your eyes to see what God is exposing. The higher you go in these organizations, the more corrupt you have to become to fit it; similar to climbing the corporate ladder. Seems like you have to engage in more corruption the higher you go. The majority of workplaces are chalked full of SSO members. SSO members can target and work collectively on people, and yes, I've experienced being a target for 'gang stalking'. I can attest to this truthfully. Moreover, I've observed when there is wrong behavior toward, or treatment of a person, they stick together in the decision, or don't say anything, so as to look the other way. I can definitely back it up with experiential facts. I think I will.

Gang stalking

The Urban dictionary refers to 'Gang Stalking' as "a form of commu-nity mobbing and organized stalking combined." It further specifies 'Workplace mobbing' as a legitimate practice which targets individuals "for revenge, jealousy, sport, or to keep them quiet." It narrows its function as "a psychological attack that can completely destroy a person's life, while leaving little or no evidence to incriminate the perpetrators. The primary targets are usually women, minorities, dissidents, whistle blowers, etc." *(Gangstalking, 2020)*. A recent article in Psychology Today painted a psychotic picture of people who are referred to as 'TI's' *(Targeted Individuals)*. While it's possible to drive a person there, Christians have a greater power to combat the emotional attacks and keep their sanity simultaneously. The emotional attack is real. Christian's read closely. We are carriers, advocates of, catalysts for, passionate about, and seekers of, and walking in truth. We don't believe in living a lie, telling a lie, hiding a lie, even though we may have done it in the past. Since we know that our enemy, the Devil, is the father of lies, our goal is to walk in truth. When we see corruption, Isaiah 58:1 *(NIV. Bible Hub, 2020)* tells us to "Shout it aloud, do not hold back. Raise your voice like a trumpet. Declare to my people their rebellion and to the descendants of Jacob their sins.." I'm imagining the goal was to shut me up and shut me down. I'm prophetic. People who are prophetic see more than they desire. If I had a decent lawyer at the time, I could have probably sued and had some people on the news. But I let God take care of them. He never misses.

Victorious victim

I know this seems like an oxymoron, but a person who is not quite sharp about what is happening to them, either because they are too busy dealing with the cares of this life, or don't have a solid prayer life, can be a victim. The Bible tells us that we are more than conquerors through Jesus Christ who loves us. *(Romans 8:37)* It also tells us we have power over all the power of the devil *(Luke 9:1-2)* But one thing I've learned in this life, if we don't know how to use our power, we become a victim mostly of our own ignorance. "My people are destroyed for lack of knowledge." *(Hosea 4:6)*

I could have not taken certain jobs in the first place, had I asked God first. I could have been fully armored according to Ephesians chapter 6, so that I would not have been so devastated by the works of the devil, if I had prayed more consistently and engaged in spiritual warfare. I could have looked at my job as an assignment from God rather than a livelihood that would jeopardize my living if I lost it. I could have been blessing those who cursed me, doing good to those who hated me and praying for those who despitefully used me. *(Matt. 5:44)* I could have looked at things for what they really were, distractions and delusions that were waiting to defeat me so I would not be a threat to Satan's kingdom by fulfilling my mandate from God. I could not have taken what was being done to me personally, it was the hidden treasure in me that the Devil was coming after to steal it or to prevent me from using it. You shall know the truth, and the truth shall make you free. *(John 8:32)* The could've, would've, should've, became can, will and shall. Once victim, now victorious by the power of the blood of Jesus. This world is not my home and my life is not my own, I've been purchased by the innocent but powerful blood of Jesus. I also realize that when I decrease, His power in me increases; especially through prayer and fasting.

5

MOST DANGEROUS GAME

How it started

Who knows how it started? Was it when I would surf the internet, namely Christian websites for challenging discussions because there was too much downtime? Was it when I wasted lots of paper printing a family calendar because an employee told me 'it was my privilege' to use the resources there? Was it because I was Black, a female, or a Christian? Better yet, was it because I was my father's child or nemesis after the back pay child support case was won by my mother? How did it start? Why did it start? Why me? All I know is, everything seemed fine until I didn't socially fit into the corporate culture. I stepped up the pace to start my own home-based business, sometimes working on my own projects when there were no projects to do at work. I know now, it was a big no, no, but it seems the persecution forced me. Then retaliation came. Looking for other jobs for the sake of peace, I found myself being black-balled. It was no longer that surveillance was enough, it was an all out mission to assassinate everything about me; my character, my associations, my God, my pending and existing relationships, my reputation, my livelihood, my social life, and moreover, my reason to exist. Everything in my world had been turned completely upside down. Even then, I felt God ordering my steps, even after the small but stupid mistakes I had made. Many times I was clueless that surveillance was taking place until the culprits began to make known indirectly what they knew about my personal life and activities. What puzzled me most was, if I was considered a criminal of some sort. If I had committed espionage or embezzlement of company funds. If I was moonlighting when the contract would not allow it, why play the game of chase, why not try me in court, have me arrested for making invitations for my friends retirement party because they knew I was good with graphics. Why not just use the money and effort it took to fail a mission in my life, and get it done and over within a court of law. Why be covert and illegal? Why do people keep saying "see you in court," if you weren't delivering a warrant or certified letter. I know . . . scare tactic. I remember cartoons and movies where they just wanted to play a little cat and mouse game with a perpetrator rather than use direct discipline. They loved the game.

On the job persecution

I had worked in Corporate America for approximately 12 years. The experiences I had were good and bad, but reasonable as it relates to my Christian beliefs, values and doctrine. It sort of goes with the package, you know, the marketing department takes ½ the day off to go to a casino, I don't gamble; secretaries tell me of their sexual relationships with their live-in boyfriends, asking my approval and agreement; I can't relate or approve. My worst persecution came from the homosexual crowd; not sure why, but I wasn't a basher, I just understood God's standards according to the Bible, lived it to the best of my ability and in my God-given ability, and it was like an all out war against the messenger. I only represent the cause of Christ, not religion, not the people who blow up abortion clinics and kill doctors who perform abortions, not homosexual terrorists or haters, not imbalanced self-proclaimed Christians who do terrible things in the name of the Lord. I was just a little young Black Christian girl from Robbins, IL, looking to make her way in the world. There were three corporations that participated in the depth of my persecution, but one main one that I will never forget, but have already forgiven. If I had a decent lawyer, no doubt, I could have sued a couple of companies *(the ones who made me sign that I wouldn't sue)* for the terrorism on the job and defamation of character. Consequently, I will always thank these companies, because they contributed tremendously to my spiritual and psychological growth; my personal experience, my testimony, and my career change. They helped me have a keener awareness of things I denied, they helped me know who my real friends were, and they forced me to go to drastic spiritual measures to stay on top. For this, I am ever grateful.

We must keep in mind that society teaches us that we're odd, flawed, and worthless if we don't jump on the bandwagon. Someone needs to take a stand against ungodliness. And those who do, are priceless. .

Company one: I remember working for an insurance company *(which will remain nameless)*, owned by a sole proprietor who later went to prison for laundering money for politics. This company was my first noteworthy experience with direct supernatural attack. I remember I worked very hard and wanted to do more creative services, but couldn't get through the political barriers. I remember the employees in that creative services group hated me so much, that it felt like a lion's den to work there and the supervisor excused their behavior by saying some adults just act like 4 or 5th graders. I would learn later that this was universal across all fields and true. I even remembered thinking, please don't put this level of stupidity on children, these are adults choosing to behave like imbeciles. It was my first major experience with the horror of surveillance. . I wanted nothing to do with that company anymore. I believe the Trinidadian executive who worked with the sole proprietor was behind the witchcraft attacks, not to mention "Mickey" taking pics of me when driving his limo while at a traffic light where I was waiting on a bus. Yes, people were taking pictures of me outside of the workplace and I especially noticed one in a limo. Imagine they needed the picture to try to curse me if they didn't have any of my possessions. It was a shock to me too. Overall, I've had whole departments wanting me out, including the company I'll tell you about later, and how far they went to get me out. Problem is, I wasn't going anywhere until God told me to go. No running from the devil; the devil was gonna have to run. Then I remember having these horrific headaches and seeing the sole proprietor *(CEO)* stand outside of the window to watch me as if I was in a zoo. Trying to see why I'm still there. I remember walking off that particular job without having another job lined up because the stress from the persecution on that job became unbearable. It seems that demonic activity escalated, the headaches became worse, and I thought, my peace is not worth enduring this hell no matter what the price.

Company two: I was a temporary worker through an agency working evenings for a fortune 500 company in the Creative Services Department. My job wasn't that creative, but it was paying some bills. I remember turning down a permanent job offer from them because I have too much creativity to do this *(I thought)* . . . I'll die of boredom. So, after not taking it, and after making the mistake of trying to print my personal family calendars and screwing up the job, wasting paper, they had employees watching me. They set up and did construction on our work area, setting up cameras. I had no problems with cameras, especially since there was nothing but work and a little boredom going on with another night shift worker, but I couldn't even straighten my slip under my skirt when no one was around without hearing some type of howling sound in the reprographics area, where males were seeing everything I did, looking at me funny when I came to use their services; behaving as if I was a criminal - monitored? By them? It seems like surveillance has its place. If a day shift worker is caught going down stairs with a printer *(which falls down a flight of stairs)*, saying he was taking it to get it fixed when really he was stealing it, why did I have to be watched so closely, and by extremely ignorant people. I'll give you an example. One night I needed to make a phone call privately, so I went into an office where I could work and have privacy at the same time. Two coworkers actually began throwing objects in the room where I was sitting and running away. I rebuked them harshly afterwards, only to discover it was reported or recorded that I went off on them, but not that they heckled, harassed, and threw objects at me. This was allowed, and I was being reprimanded. About eight or nine years after leaving that company, one of the reprographics guys watching me, who probably saw under my dress, apologized profusely to me in the parking lot of a Jewel near my home. I remembered him trying to date me and me thinking horrendous thoughts that this imbecile was assigned to watch every move I made.

I left that company to go to another which is where the story catches on fire.

Company three: I remember having a great interview with this company, but seeing my potential supervisor and others on a conference call because she couldn't give me the word until after the meeting. I thought, I hope no black ball is rolling here. I would never make the same mistakes I had made in the past *(as if they were horrendous)* because this is a bit of a dream job for me. I absolutely love working in creative services. A former employee who worked with me at the previous company put in a good word for me there and eventually told me that she knew something was brewing at the old company. Word had gotten all the way to her, but she would never tell me what exactly was brewing. Before I go on, I'm going to tell you some incidents that happened to me.

Off the job terrorism

As my last days there were quickly approaching, I found myself not only being followed everywhere I went publicly, but also privately. I've

32

felt that I was seen naked and on a screen with an audience, possibly a secret society or witchcraft audience. When did they get the chance to wiretap or bug with small cameras for video and sound? At work. I worked evenings from 4 pm to 12 midnight so during summers I would take a walk around Buckingham Fountain or the lake just to watch the water, relax, ease my mind, and go back within the hour. I remember one specific day when I took a lunch walk and a Caucasian male walked ahead of me, stood at the light and pretended to be speaking in tongues. I knew later that it was to get my attention and we had what could have been a fruitful conversation about believing God for relationships except, when we approached my work, he held me outside almost 20 minutes longer. I had left my cell phone and glasses, and they must not have been finished with the wiring. The reason I know is because, after an accident on my way to work one day, with a taxi driver who bumped me from behind, I had a weird experience when I pursued him fixing the damage he had done. He said to me once "you never use your cell phone". How did he know? I also remember this perverted security guard who was always trying to hit on me, tell me he likes my glasses, keep wearing them. He said this with a grin and a smile that wasn't just a friendly greeting. I suspected they put tiny cameras on my glasses so that everything I see, they see; going to the bathroom, taking your clothes off and everything else.

I also remember my car was followed everywhere. I used to park in the garage in a high rise building downtown and walk across the street to my job. I remembered as soon as I parked one day, two angry looking men were coming in the same direction as my car, but I had to keep moving on to work. After work, I had a flat tire that night on the way home and couldn't get help until 2 a.m. from a police officer who kept circling and telling me I had to move my car. I remember seeing the parking lot attendant at my dad's house one day, and when I looked to talk to him later, he no longer worked for the company. He had something to tell me; he indicated this once. Then I couldn't find him. How coincidental.

Sometimes people would meet me at a destination before I arrived. I remember taking my grandma to a WalMart or Kmart and a huge Black man who was right at the entrance followed us intently until I noticed. When I turned around to confront him, he went another way. My grandmother acknowledged what happened, but again, this was after I decided to be quiet and stop addressing everything I saw, and allow others to see for themselves.

Here's another mistake I made that resulted in the next form of stalking and terrorizing; I used my corporate American express card for personal purchases and one particular time was 45 days late with payment. It was then that mysterious people were standing at cash registers when I checked out with anything. Once I paid for a 2 day cruise with which to take my mom as a birthday gift. Again, I had the money but needed to use the card to reserve the spot. A whole crew followed this time. I encountered a sort of paparazzi experience with cameras on me in the water, on the boat, practically for every morsel of food I put in my mouth. I remember being asked by the company to upgrade to a bigger boat but couldn't afford it, so many of my stalking terrorists got sea sick from the rocking of the boat. I could hear them vomiting in the cabin next to me. I also remember sitting at a dinner table in the dining area and the unwanted guests sitting with us, trying to start a conversation and ending it with "see you in court", for no reason. This was the second time I'd heard this. It had nothing to do with the conversation and it was told to my mom this time. Before, a co worker at company number 2 told me this same statement 'see you in court', a week before I was leaving the company. I thought, if I were doing something illegal, please, I'm willing to take the responsibility and suffer my own consequences. Maybe people just wanted to have a little fun with me because it seemed like I was a mindless clueless Christian. I was a target who wasn't losing her mind fast enough. I remember writing the 10 page report to my employer of company #3 about the level of harassment I endured. I remember them denying everything except the sexual harassment accusation of a homosexual male employee and I remember saying I didn't need the retaliation – they must have told him, or he must have heard because it got worse.

I remember getting so tired of the stalking, the harassment, the antagonistic efforts until one day I just said "Oh God, how long". I brought a mini tape recorder to work that day and, coincidentally, it was the day I was let go from my job WITH a package. I thought, if I was grossly insubordinate or horrific as an employee, they would not have given me a package. And this was during the time I was in the middle of purchasing a house, and had completed the paperwork with the mortgage company. Can you believe someone was trying to stop it? Probably because the set up would have me jobless until I changed careers; only I didn't know at the time. The realtor went from being super friendly to cutting her eyes at me the next day – repeating something I had said on the phone to someone else the previous day, which was that I would probably change jobs in the spring. I was purchasing this house in the winter.

I remember how coworkers on this job pulled the same stunt, having access to my personal email on hotmail, and me writing preaching letters to them *(but addressed to myself)*. It was my way to quietly show them they were caught spying. One day when I came to work, a coworker whispered to another coworker about wanting to read the letter, and another coworker told her, she has to open it first *(referring to me)*. I didn't understand how people could collectively be part of my persecution, or even wanted to. Did anyone have any dignity in themselves? Was anybody honest or caring or compassionate like I am? Is everyone around me corrupt? The day I lost this job, I heard the same coworker who was reading my emails on Hotmail say, "I'm gonna miss our day meetings." Since I worked nights, they had special meetings during the day. They knew I was being let go, before I did. Isn't that amazing. Whatever organization(s) was behind me singled out, had many people involved; the ones I saw, and the ones who came by to see me. It's like they were looking in a cage at a rare species. How coincidental. However, this did get dangerous to my soundness of mind and well-being.

I sat after church in the car with my cousin talking to her about some problems that I was encountering emotionally. We talked for about an hour. I guess I wasn't the moving target they were looking for that day, so a van pulled up in front of where we were parked and a guy got out of the van with a fake sheriff's badge on his jacket to scare me. It did initially, I thought, are they coming to get me right here, right now? He gave this eerie smile and got back in the van and they took off. I didn't understand this. Was I in trouble with the law? Don't they just get a warrant and arrest you? What was this game being played? Was it Greek, Wiccan, Cult, or Mason? Or was it just the actions of plain old corrupt, underground, secret society?

I can recall an account of two African American female employees who were terrified at Company 3. One came to me to tell me how weird people were behaving there and feared losing her job. She told me of a conversation she had with another female about all the things they encountered, and how the other co-worker mentioned "if they want to fire me, they'll have to walk me out." And that's just what happened to her. It's as if they responded to her challenge. Now this young lady, we'll call her Jane, came quickly to me, eyes big as silver dollars, practically sneaking around the corner to talk to me, and she told me of the incident that happened to her friend whom we'll call Terri. She told me how she had a hard time getting another job, her gas was cut off, she was a single parent, and had to cook in a toaster oven, among other hardships she experienced. Jane's whole disposition was desperation and fear. She got out of that company as fast as she could. She finally disappeared. Little did I realize, I would be the next target.

On February 9, 2001, the day I moved into my recently purchased home. Before I could get into the door I had two visitors; the previous owner, and one unidentified man with an FBI cap on his head. It seems he was coercing the previous owner against his will to do this but he came with a disinterested expression on his face. The unidentified man with the FBI paraphernalia walks up and says "which one of you is Yvette Hill". How the conversation went after that I can't remember, I only know that nothing scared me at this point, and I believed it was intended to be yet another scare tactic. My mom and grandma were with me at that time with the Rental truck. You guys, this was a fake FBI.

You won't believe – No one did

This was a really strange one, but at least in 4 different churches me, my mom, and my grandma attended as visitors, the lights went off and on 3 times. As if it was one for each of us. Even the pastors didn't know what was going on, but a select group of people did. Apostles, watch who you appoint in your church as leaders. You may need to do background checks on some. Make sure they are not part of corrupt Secret Societies. They cannot serve God and Baal.

Company 4: Miraculously, I got a new job after company 3 'Let me go with a package'. My boss was openly homosexual, but my coworkers weren't, so I didn't know anyone openly homosexual but my boss. I didn't care either, but suddenly I started experiencing things there. The black ball was rolling again. Looking for a job prior to company 3, I remember interviewing at a different company across the street from my previous job and having a great interview. When I left, I saw consultants from Company 3 getting off an elevator on the same floor I had just left, with large visible cameras. The 2nd interview I was called for was cold and calloused. I remember commenting to a co worker at Company 3 that I had a personal prejudice against my own kind for a long time because my experience with many Black women, especially after they attained positions of power, is that they become controlling, cutthroat, backstabbing, and just not friendly; very difficult to work with, work for, and satisfy. Society has a name for it; it's called "Angry Black Woman." It happened that I would have been assisting a Black woman at the potential new job, who refreshingly seemed not to fit that stereotype. It seemed promising, but I believe 'stalkers' from Company 3 went to this potential employer, just like everything and everyone else whom I valued, and let them hear the audio of my prejudiced concerns to my colleague. I'm thinking it was just a private conversation, but it was recorded and shown. The nature of questions at the second interview reflected this. I knew they had been spoken to, and I probably didn't have a chance. I didn't get that job.

Finally, when I landed at Company 4, they initially had me working with another young lady into the night shift – so I was in training and we shared the work. One day she told me how a guy in technology shared with her information about an executive who always had porn on his desktop – meaning they monitored what he was doing and saw the porn. I told her yeah, I know about the monitoring that goes on in corporate settings and how it's not supposed to be gossiped around the office, but they do that. The next day, to my surprise, my co-worker was relieved of her duties and I was left to work the night shift alone. All the work suddenly piled on and I couldn't manage it because the tools they hired me with were now fading because of a slow work flow during training. I couldn't produce quality for too much quantity and now I was pink slipped. I thought, this wasn't the agreement. You hired me with help, then removed the help, then say i'm not adequately performing, yet have me train the next person – why would you trust me if i'm being fired? Then I tried to figure out what this set-up was all about. On a side note: I still obeyed God's word, blessed my employers in prayer, and maintained a great attitude by staying in the secret place. I even created a brochure for the department, as a gift, before I walked out the door.

One day prior to all this drama, I came to work. I told a coworker I had a dream about him. He previously told me how he liked nature and bears, etc, but I dreamt I saw him in a ballerina uniform, and how funny the dream was. As I relayed the dream to him, at first he laughed, then gave me this evil look. I thought, 'Me and my goofy dreams.' I was just trying to get to know my coworkers and show them my funny side, but he didn't think it was so funny. Soon my boss would enter the room as if a ballerina dancer. I thought it was kind of strange, I mean, why was he doing that. Then, while working with me and expressing I was doing a good job on a project, he rubbed my back and snapped my bra strap. I thought it was extremely inappropriate, and why does my supervisor think it's ok to do that. But I had been abused so much, mistreated so much, persecuted so much, I just felt like it was a way of life. Nobody was going to listen to me, protect and defend me, look out for me. I felt like I'd be a victim forever until God did something about it, but I wasn't walking away again. Never! This is my livelihood, I thought. With an after-thought that God is truly my source. If I have to record something, then I will, but I was going nowhere – because the next place would be worse. Some of the interns would even act extremely unprofessional with me, putting their buttocks in my face while I worked, and talking condescendingly. Again, I looked for mature professionals and couldn't find them. I ran into a coworker from another department in an elevator who mentioned to me about the coworker I dreamt about. She said he had invited many people to come to his partner's concert at a prestigious downtown Catholic church where his partner was the choir director. She asked me if I attended, I said I never knew about it. She said 'didn't you know he was homosexual?' I told her "I had no idea". Do you know that it took years after I lost that job to realize that God Himself showed me in a dream through this ballerina image of my coworker's sexual preference – though he wanted me to believe he was a masculine nature man. By me innocently telling him the dream, he thought I was mocking him, I assumed, told my boss, and the harassment began. Ladies and gentlemen reading this book, I was persecuted for my dream and I didn't even realize it. I should have learned from Joseph, not to tell my dreams to everyone. In spite of what people show us, God shows us the truth. By the way, it didn't matter to me that my coworker was homosexual, I don't have homophobia. It only mattered to me that we got along, worked together, accepted our differing personalities, and respected each other. But God does things the way He wants, and it's all for a reason.

A funny thing happened

One thing about my spiritual senses or gift of discerning spirits is that it sharpened. I could always tell when it was 'one of them'. Not the person, but the principality behind the person. No one could really deceive me except maybe the initial confrontation I had with the fake tongue talking man at the lake. It took me a while because I was so hungry to find someone who was as devout a Christian as I, who believed the way I believed, and could relate and identify with me.

At Christmas time, I received a Christmas Card from one of the executives at Company 3 which actually used the words 'Christ' and 'Christmas', as opposed to 'Happy Holidays' and 'Winter Wonderland', so I thought, 'is she a real Christian?' I wrote a letter to her asking that very question, and though she never returned my answer, she greeted me in the ladies room and spoke vaguely to me – but I understood, I had been recorded in this very bathroom, and I didn't want to get her in trouble for associating with me. She smiled and walked out.

There was a Company 3 picnic that I attended with my aunt and her 2 kids as my guests at the time. When I arrived to check in, there was a raffle drawing to which I was given a ticket. This same smiling lady was supervising the raffle ticket table where the young female employees were working. My mind was conditioned to believe I could never win anything, so to saved myself the disappointment, I gave my ticket to my aunt to increase her chances of winning something. I just wanted to relax, enjoy the peace for the moment, sit in the sun, let the kids enjoy and go home. I inevitably spent some time sitting by myself on the grass to just watch things and meditate on God. As they continued under the tent to call out winning numbers, my cousin came running out to look for me. Excited and breathless he said "Yvette, Yvette, they called your number, you won the grand prize." I said what? No! you sure? He said come on, you gotta get it! So he pulls me in the tent and pushes me to go to the front. I really did! I had won a beautiful $900.00 Camcorder with all the bells and whistles. My aunt said she didn't think it was fair to take it because it was my ticket so she let me rightfully claim my prize. I thought, wait a minute, all these negative things this company has been doing to me and suddenly I get something nice out of it. I couldn't believe it. But it was true.

As we sat flaunting and chirping over this big huge win while sitting at the pool, the same executive smiling lady came there to sunbathe quietly, and I could tell was eavesdropping and happy for me at the same time. I looked at her as if to say 'you must have been behind this' and looked away, because again, I respected boundaries and was unselfish enough not to want anyone suffering because of me. A photographer took a picture of me at the momentous occasion and said something puzzling to me to this day. He said 'you made history'. I never really understood what he meant, and although I asked him to repeat what he said and why he just said the same thing again with no real explanation. I thought 'he probably sees that I'm surviving, not losing my mind, fighting back, and winning. 'He probably knows what's going on more than I do.'

The Church

I remember thinking there is a nest of witches in this place – can't you see it? The particular church I attended at the time was highly favored by me, but some of the people were not the brightest. Somehow my adversaries had gotten through to my church and were trying to defame my character there. It seemed they wanted to shred every single avenue of my life into pieces so I would have nothing to live for, and ultimately, become suicidal. I remember the level of anxiety increased when I saw this happening. I invited an Indian friend I met online to come and visit my church. He never came, but told me what the message was about. I went out on a date with him, as I tripped and fell on an unseen step, he looked up as if to see if they got that on camera without even trying to help me up right away.

I joined the intercessory prayer group at my church. As I tried to explain my suffering to the head of that auxiliary, she tried to make me look like I was crazy, when I had simply undergone a great deal of stress and what I considered more 'witchcraft' psychological attacks. I remember the pastor preaching against having so called 'friends', referencing boyfriends or girlfriends, as carnal people know it. Suddenly two female members sat by me, one on each side, as if to say something wasn't right about me. When the pastor remarked on not having 'friends' of the opposite sex, as if one is automatically in fornication, one questioned me during the service if I have any 'friends' like that. Today it would be called "friends with benefits". But I lived a holy life. I was so insulted. Here I am living upright, maybe guilty of always trying to run away from or avoid conflict, and feeling lonely, but I was pure in the sexual area of my life. No porn, no boyfriends, no sugar daddies, no baby daddies, and I was being treated like I had just become a Christian yesterday. I have been an ordained minister since 1991. Another time, I walked in one day to go to the Sunday service. As I walked to the restroom, a young lady *(minister's wife)* stood at the door of the bathroom, saw me, and immediately spoke in tongues as if she had just seen a witch or been in company with the devil himself. I thought, 'what rumor is going on around here?' 'what is being said?'

I finally went for counseling at my church. They had just hired a woman who held a Doctorate in Psychology and I had hoped that a real, mature and professional Christian could really help me sort through this. I went to my appointment. She introduced herself and showed me a tape recorder to alert me that they like to record sessions for their records and for legal purposes. I approved. She then walked away, saying she would be back. She was gone for about 10 min. and I decided to look at the Music Cd she had on her desk, as I was always looking for suggestions on good worship music. As she reentered the room, it was like a Tasmanian devil had stepped in. She snatched the cd from me and scolded me never to touch anything on her desk because there could be personal private information. I explained that I was just looking at the music cd to see what kind of songs may be of interest to me. She didn't care, she was no longer polite, and proceeded to ask me incriminating questions. I mentioned the situation that happened with a man at my job who persuaded me into giving him my business card after he set me up with this sad emergency they claimed to have, about not having a projector for a meeting the next day. As soon as I handed it to him, asking if they outsource to other companies he said "gotcha", smiled and called someone. I would have never done this, but to my amazement the counselor asked "were you dating that man"? I surprisingly answered "No, what makes you think that?" Someone had gotten to her. There was no mention from me of having relations or relational problems, just problems of being depressed and bullied by folks I knew and didn't know. It's like she was accusing me so she can say the source of my problems was from living in sin. I thought, 'who talked to her?' Well, that session was the only one and it was a disaster. To top things off, the so-called leader of the prayer warriors of the church -of which I was very dedicated- had been listening at the door, and was pretending to be cleaning around the door. They suspected me for something, and I had no idea what they were expecting, but was truly disappointed that they would believe anything anybody told them, that I didn't confess myself. That this was my church family and they were suddenly against me. My whole existence was crumbling away with almost everyone around me that I loved and respected, and now my church family would be soon disappearing from my favorite list. Family didn't believe me, thought I was stressed out or going crazy, but now the church didn't believe in me, thought I was some kind of undercover hypocrite. Employees were harassing me on and off the grounds. What was I to do?

Then one day I got a little ray of hope; my pastor at the time, didn't openly but discreetly walked by me during the service, told me "I know you're a true woman of God" and kept going. Why he wouldn't say it into the microphone to save my reputation, I don't know, but about 40 pounds thinner, and 10 feet taller in the Spirit, I needed to hear that. Yes, I had fasted and prayed for a month to get through this.

Eventually, I left that church to go to the headquartered church which was closer to home and the beloved accusing sisters followed me there. Soon I had a female prophet looking at me as if I had two heads. She introduced herself to me, but behaved very strangely. I thought, wow, even so-called gifted Christians are so easily misled to believe lies. Their gifts can't possibly be working well. Motivation must be by their own flesh, rather than the Spirit of the Living God. I know too much about God and people to not give people a chance. The gift of discerning Spirits will show you everything you need to know – use it!

Scariest moments

As fearless as I am, I must admit there were a few scary moments, while most were simply annoying, unbelievable, and simply thought to be unrealistic. One such moment was when I walked outside my workplace at around 1 a.m. to go to the next building where my car was parked. I recognized a day shift co-worker standing at the window looking in from a distance and my disbelief that she was standing there. A limo suddenly pulled off from down the street to the entrance of that building as if waiting for me. It put on a show, skidding while taking off fast and coming to a screeching stop. I had a camera with me at the time and just kind of positioned it so I could take a picture of the license plate while walking toward the door. I remember thinking 'are they going to finally abduct me, shoot me, what?' It was all to scare me, but immediately, after the incident, I decided to take a life insurance policy out on myself because I really wasn't sure what else these people would do.

Unwanted guests

Another scary moment was, after I'd left that job and went to Company 4, my mom called me one night at work to report to me that a limo had pulled up to the house. A Caucasian man got out of the car and knocked on the door asking for me. She told them I wasn't there and they insisted on her opening the door. She refused to let them in, telling them I wasn't there and eventually they went away. As she peered out of the window, she could see the limo, however, she didn't see that it was a police car, or even an unmarked squad car. I was aware my stalkers knew where I lived, but coming to my house again, for what? Knowing everything they knew, they had to know I wasn't home, thus another scary thing for my family. I'm glad the 'Medea' didn't come out of my mom or there would have been another type of war.

6

HOW I SURVIVED

onquering the covert through prayer, fasting and obedience
to God
The Holy Spirit had given me instructions on how to conquer
this outrageous giant monster that had stepped into my world and tried
to squeeze the very life out of me. This stalking had me terrorized,
paranoid, and wondering if it would ever go away.

God specifically instructed me to fast, pray, consecrate myself and
meditate on His word. That should be a regular thing in this Christian
life, but I had to do it on steroids. I did just that. For at least a month I
fasted half of it – drinking only a glass of juice at night for dinner. At
lunchtime, I would go to my car and listen to the Bible on CD and just
fall asleep with it. I had an hour. Forget the working lunch. I was taking
this one for the whole month. I chose a specific passage of scripture
to meditate on; Psalms 37. I specifically focused on 5 verses of which
I meditated, recited, remembered, and stood on. They are vs 1-2, 7,
10, 23-24, 35-36. I needed reinforcement that God was on my side no
matter who was against me. But I also needed to know that God was
going to defend me and bring me out of this victoriously. At one point
I thought I would lose my mind. No one understood. No one I spoke

to had endured something of this nature; and when they saw what was happening, they couldn't do anything about it but become hostile or complain; this wasn't helping me at all. I had to STAND on God's word.

Draw from the power of God within

This was the first time in my life when I realized that everything I needed to not just survive, but conquer this, was already inside me. All the teaching I received as a child, all the scriptures I had memorized, all of the teaching I engaged in myself, all of the prayers, all of the confirmations of God's word being performed in my life – even through prophecy, all that I had learned was an actual treasure chest planted inside me. Nothing external helped. Everything internally sustained me. It was just AMAZING! God's grace was truly sufficient. His strength was really being matured through my weakness. I almost couldn't believe it myself. This was a new level of attack, this was witchcraft, and I was above it because of my God strengthening and loving me. No one can EVER tell me God doesn't exist, or that there are many roads that lead to the God of the universe, the creator of all mankind, the intelligent designer of heaven and earth and everything in the firmament, stratosphere and atmosphere. He LIVES!!! And is very much alive in His people. They just don't realize how much.

Disconnecting from all unhealthy worldly systems

We in America are like programmed robots. We are mesmerized by all the technology and entertainment that could bombard our lives if we allow it. We have all kinds of gates with which spiritual elements *(and natural elements)* can enter. Eyes, ears, nose, mouth, and the other entry.

Eyes

Eyes are the windows to your soul. Matthew 6:22-23 *(NIV. Bible. Bible Hub, 2020)*

22 "The eye is the lamp of the body. If your eyes are healthy,[a] your whole body will be full of light. 23 But if your eyes are unhealthy,[b] your whole body will be full of darkness. If then the light within you is darkness, how great is that darkness! The short of this is. . . I couldn't watch tv or movies. I couldn't do any secular internet. I couldn't let just anything come into my window - the windows of my soul. I had to filter things so that I could strictly stay focused on Jesus. He is, has been and always will be my very present help in trouble.

Ears

"So then faith *comes* by hearing, and hearing by the word of God" (*NKJV. Bible. Romans 10:17*). Ears are gates of which things can enter, but cannot exit. The things we hear are not to be taken lightly and should be filtered by the Holy Ghost. When a child grows up hearing things like "you're ugly, stupid, won't amount to anything, good for nothing," the child grows up believing that and many times manifests this because he/she internalized what they heard. Don't believe what your critics or enemies say completely. If they are not speaking God's promises to you - calling those things that be not as though they were; esteeming you even higher than themselves, you may have to turn a deaf ear during this crucial time. You also need to avoid gossiping on the phone or in personal conversations. Gossip, or just people gathering mud on people, used to hurt me, and I could literally feel the bitter effect of it in my gut. You need to listen to sermons, worship music, edifying and building Christian communication, exhortation. You can't afford to listen to your favorite secular "cut' or things that simply appeal to your flesh. You are at war for your soul. You must stay focused.

Nose

"All the while my breath is in me, and the spirit of God is in my nostrils" (*NKJV. Bible. Job 27:3*). You'd be surprised how all of your senses are affected when you're in a spiritual warfare. The Bible references nostrils mostly when it comes to sin - it stinks to Him, worship is a sweet smell to him. We are just like our Heavenly Father. If you are around smokers, you might want to avoid it and clear your atmosphere. Aromas can actually prove to be therapeutic.

Mouth

"What goes into someone's mouth does not defile them, but what comes out of their mouth, that is what defiles them." *(Matthew 15:11)* David, the king and Psalmist once said "put a watch over the doorpost of my mouth." He knew he needed more control over the tongue; which by the way, no man can tame; however, we must realize how powerful our words are. "For out of the abundance of the heart, the mouth speaketh. And so a man thinketh, so is he." *(KJV. Bible. Proverbs 23:7)* It was extremely important that no doubt, fear, unbelief, anxiety, worry, came into my heart, or out of my mouth. It was vital that I trusted the Lord enough and gave absolutely no room for these enemies of my faith.

I Had A Dream

I remember while fasting and praying in this catastrophic stalking, I had a dream one night. In the dream I was sitting in court *(which was something they always said "see you in court")* and, along with others, names were being called to be tried or convicted of a crime. As I sat, expecting to hear my name called, my chair began to rise. Next thing you know, I was on a cliff's edge continually rising above the courthouse. I rose so high, I could almost see clouds below me as I looked down on the tiny courthouse. I worried that they would call my name and I would not hear it, so I quickly slid down the mountain to find myself back in the same courthouse. I walked to the desk where the lady called the names of everyone being tried and asked "did you call my name?" She asked what my name was, I told her and she combed the list only to not find my name at all. She remarked, "Your name isn't on the list, Next!" I insisted, I said "oh yes, that's why I'm here", she coldly said "Next!" again. The Lord revealed to me at that moment that He was placing me above the circumstances and beyond reproach. No one can or will accuse me of any crime. It was like something in me broke and I was freed. I didn't have to wonder anymore if I did anything to deserve this horrible mission on me, I didn't have to fear anything or anyone. Psalm 37 was in effect, and all I needed to do was stand on God's word. He is my avenger, He is my defender, He is my protector, He is my refuge and fortress according to Psalm 91. There was nothing too difficult for Him, thus, there was nothing too difficult for me. That meant everything to me. I awakened a new person.

Another funny thing Happened

Right before I started writing this book, I was late going to work and was stopping at a Walgreens. I really should have been at work at the time but I promised the kids candy and owed them – so I went. At the entrance was a well-groomed, clean looking Caucasian man with Jeans, a jacket, and a sign that said he was clean, drug free, and had a family. I wasn't sure if the sign said 'homeless' or 'will work for food', but as I approached the door, it was as if he suddenly recognized me and was blinking his eyes and looking down so I wouldn't recognize him. Initially, I thought nothing of it except 'how do we know you're drug free; you look like you can work for anybody right now.' Then I thought, well, I'll give him a couple bucks when I come out. When I came out, he was gone completely. I thought, 'why would he run away?' And why was he seeming embarrassed or didn't want me to recognize him? My mind triggered. He looked like the young man I saw and talked to at the lake, who walked me back to the company site and detained me while they were still rigging my cell phone and personal belongings. Is someone else a target that he's assigned to and I just happened to be in the right place at the right time? Did he see my angels in the spirit realm? What is really going on?

Stop telling everybody

When all these unbelievable incidents occurred, I started telling the people closest to me. Those people included my mom, a former co-worker, and a couple of uncles. The first things they said irritated my soul. Nobody believed me. They perceived my experiences as only imagined, and that I was just exhausted. Let's see. The definition of exhausted according to Merriam Webster's online dictionary is: depleted of energy : extremely tired. That, I was. Able to create stories like this? You can't make this up. I was creative, but not that much. I even had a relative clap 3 times and look at me to see what my reaction would be. I honestly think they believed I was going crazy. Without a solid relationship with God, I don't believe I would have made it. Nobody believed me when I told them I worked with witches, warlocks, and sorcerers; when people were imitating my every move and word even when I was not in their presence. Nobody believed that people were stalking me in an effort to make me paranoid or afraid to be caught alone, that people would call my name out of the blue, as I walked to my destinations or that people were trying to drug me, follow me, manipulate my life, Black list me, follow me on vacation, take pictures of me, and manipulate new relationships so they could back me into a corner that I could never escape from. I became silent. I said "they will see for themselves". Then, the day came. My grandmother and mother saw that we were being followed through the store. They saw flashes from picture taking at restaurants. They saw people recording me at random restaurants with their phones almost like paparazzi style. They even followed my mom when she drove my car, possibly thinking it was me. She had the temper and would fearlessly confront, slam car doors when they parked too close, or whatever offensive intrusive thing the assigned stalkers would do. They no longer thought I was crazy because they saw. I was relieved at that point. The most important people to me now understood.

Listen to the voice of God

This next situation is one in which you hear about happening to others, but don't expect to ever happen to you. Our small department was scheduled to go on a celebratory dinner for doing so well. The creative services department had set it up to meet at a local restaurant downtown Chicago-Catch 35. I arrived a little late and they had not yet ordered anything but drinks, so I sat at the table and took a tiny sip of the water they served me. In a matter of seconds, I suddenly felt lightheaded: like I was going to faint. I excused myself and went to the ladies room. I entered a stall and sat down because I felt like I was going to fall down. I prayed a quick prayer for protection when immediately the Holy Spirit told me not to leave anything I drink unattended, there was going to be an attempt to spike my drink. I only had water; they knew I didn't drink alcohol, but, where I came from, I understood that people can spike candy, food, or anything else if they really want to poison or drug you. I didn't want to leave the stall until I felt sure of my ability to stand erect and not feel dizzy. Another woman was in the ladies room holding lotion and asked me "would you like some hand cream", after I had washed my hands. The Holy Spirit told me that the lotion can contain drugs that can go straight into the bloodstream to activate what I had already felt I had taken in. I'm sure you're saying, now, I know she's crazy. I'll show you I'm not. Being a teacher of teens for over 15 years, I've heard many drug stories. Not only can street drugs be ingested in foods *(marijuana brownies, cookies, gummies)*, smoked, injected, in bath salts *(Synthetic cannabinoids)*, inhaled, put in the form of liquids for vaporizers, taken orally in powders and pills; students have been known to use street drugs being put on band aids, and stickers directly on the skin that can go into the bloodstream. Even LSD can be painted onto small squares of paper that people lick or swallow. I wasn't educated from the streets, but by the Holy Spirit. The gift of discerning spirits was at work again. I stated I didn't want the lotion. She insisted again. I had to finally tell her that I had my own, and no, thank you. I left the ladies room and went back to my seat at the restaurant table with my coworkers. By then, another employee had left, who originally entered as I was going to the ladies room. The Holy Spirit said "they saturated your drink with more drugs, don't drink." Immediately, they were ready to toast. Everyone grabbed their glass of wine; I took my water and participated in the toast. They drank. I put my glass down and continued talking to a coworker after they took their sips. Then, the very thing I knew would happen, happened. "Drink your water", a co worker said. "No, I'm fine." "Go ahead, drink the water." It was sooooo obvious to me that I hadn't gone along with the plan. After about 5 minutes, 2 culprit co workers walk out for a chat. I laughed inside. 'They're not carrying me out on a stretcher,' I thought.

After we ordered our food, which I felt was safe, I blessed it when it arrived and ate with conviction and discernment. "Aah," I uttered, 'I got through that safely,' I thought. Now it was time for dessert. The co-worker across from me wanted to order, and, in Corporate America dining, you share desserts. The Holy Spirit told me it was safe only to share the dessert with someone else they liked. Hey, this situation was no joke, and could have been a matter of life/death, or sanity/insanity. God warns us before anything happens, then empowers us to counterattack through prayer. Never ignore the voice of the Lord. Never doubt God is speaking. I left that night with a full stomach, a sound mind, an angry devil, and a victory won.

7

TREASURE IN EARTHEN VESSELS

What you need is inside
I explain it to people like this; God made everyone with
a backpack - spiritually and literally. What do I mean?
Sometimes we desperately look for help, grappling for straws, going
down for the third time because it appears that life problems and
pressures are squeezing the life out of us. Fear creeps in, followed by
anxiety, depression, oppression, and weariness. These are the perfect
storm ingredients for a person to give up on life or worse, getting sick.
Japanese author, Goi Nasu said "An entire sea of water can't sink a ship
unless it gets inside the ship". You must protect your peace by not
allowing certain thought processes, habits, and negative emotions inside.
It is important to realize you have what you need inside you; the contents
of the 'God spot' for those who know God. You can win this battle. Side
note: those who don't know God still have God's gifts and callings in
their lives: they just haven't discovered it, don't know how to use it, or
haven't developed them. He never takes His gifts back, whether you are
an Atheist, Agnostic, Anti-Christ, or Pantheistic. When you open the
door to your heart and allow Christ to come into a personal relationship
with you, those things are activated, directed and developed properly.

When one prays to the Father in the authority and name of Jesus Christ, there is an activation of God's power. When you read, understand and memorize the word of God, you have your weapons of spiritual warfare. When you learn to worship God in the secret place, you are protected. Effectual fervent prayer will definitely change things or change you.

Doubt and compromise are your worst enemies

This is not the time to throw in the towel and run. This is the time to fight. What would the Israelites have done if David had no courage to kill Goliath? The entire army was scared. They didn't know what they were going to do. God did it His way. Because David the Sheep Herder had already exercised his fight with other opponents, he had a confidence in God that this was just another day for victory that he anticipated with boldness. He knew he was not depending on his own strength; but he depended on his God-given strategy. His faith had been so sharpened through his continual use of it. Every human being on this planet is given the same measure of faith. Like muscles are developed from exercise, so must your faith in God be exercised. You must believe that God will deliver you, and give yourself no other way to think. The Bible declares that whoever calls on the name of the Lord will be delivered. Your faith is being tested. Will you pass the test?

Compromise is a faith killer. When a believer compromises his faith, he or she is taking shortcuts to comfort themselves. Rather than fasting and praying to stay focused for the miraculous turnaround, some believers will resort to the world system of handling trouble. Street or prescribed drugs, alcohol, fornication or adultery, bad company, vengeance, excessive eating, porn addictions; the list goes on. How can God work on your behalf if you are going to take matters into your own hands? It's like telling God to look the other way, while you resort to trivial, carnal, worldly, and sometimes demonic ways to handle your problems. You will find yourself in worse trouble. The problem may be prolonged or become more complicated. Don't make your situation worse. Don't mock God. Trust Him. Don't test Him. It's not your place.

'This one's on me' says the Lord

God knows how much you can bear. Remember when King Jehoshaphat became afraid while being surrounded by enemies of Israel: Ammon and Moab surrounding them on Mount Seir? He referred to them as a 'great multitude' coming against him and his people. He was sure they were not prepared to win this battle. Not only did he want to remind God of the previous victories He allowed them to experience to get into the promised land, but he demonstrated trust despite his own human frailties. God gave them specific instructions earlier, not to fight them; and now, here they come. He knew there was absolutely no way the Israelites could win the battle without God's intervention. He resorted to prayer, praise and worship and received instructions from God to just simply "Be Still and know that I am God". This is a word for you. Whatever, or whoever comes against you may seem greater than you. They may truly be larger than you in number, status, position, or rank. One thing is certain; no one is greater than the Most High. Greater is He that is in you, than he that is in the world (*KJV. Bible. Bible Hub, 2020*)

8

THE REWARDS

Sharpened gifts

After this whole ordeal with the aggressive spiritual attacks against me, I determined not to take it personally, and I noticed a wonderful thing came out of this. Spiritual gifts were sharper within me. I never felt I had those gifts, but it's a package deal. I had been taught about all nine supernatural gifts according to I Corinthians 12, back in 1991, when I was ordained into the ministry. This was a whole different level, and a level to which God believed I was ready to elevate. It was also a level that validated the phrase "higher levels, higher devils." Ephesians 6 tells us about spiritual wickedness in high places. My spiritual hearing had increased, my gift of discerning of spirits increased, faith *(for God's protection)*, diverse kinds of tongues, and word of wisdom gifts. I realized how these gifts protect us, whether through warning of the inevitable, which prepares us; or avoidance of things to come. Fighting the good fight of faith means you are going to be tested, tried, and proven. No child of God will be able to get around the test they must pass. Get out of your mind that the term average Christian exists. You are a spirit, you have a soul, and you live in a physical body. After your spirit is born again you must 'work it out.' You need to be fed, nurtured, and exercised, so that you can grow. The Bible says "work out your own salvation with fear and trembling." *(Philippians 2:12)* Don't take your Christian walk lightly. If a human baby is born and just lies there: no milk, no movement, no communication, no removal of waste and toxins, something is seriously wrong. That child is a vegetable or is in a vegetative state or stillborn.

Keep in mind; there are more spirits on this planet than people. What is not seen with the naked, natural eye, is really what's real and eternal. Whereas, what we see is temporary and fading away. Even mankind, once immortal, became mortal because of sin. Remember when Satan came in the form of a serpent in the Garden of Eden? When he deceived Eve, who, at first, expressed an interest in obeying God's orders. Tempting her to eat the fruit of the tree of the knowledge of Good and Evil, Satan rebutted "you shall not die. You shall be as gods; knowing good and evil." Guess what, immediately Human DNA and genetics completely changed, and humans had shorter and shorter life spans: even until now. People are dying before even being born. Mortality was never the will of God from the beginning. Thank God that He became flesh, came to His created earth, and fulfilled His mission to save us from the wages and bondage of sin. Took the keys to death, hell, and the grave and redeemed us from the curse of the Mosaic Law. He restored a close relationship once more, for those who believe in the Lord Jesus. And has given us the promise of eternal life and a future of a new heaven, new earth, new Jerusalem, and new body. Search the scriptures.

The indwelling of the Holy Spirit allows us to function supernaturally. The Bible declares that the cares of this life "choke" the word of God out of us. Daily life can be so distracting. The daily demands of work, family, ministry, community, school, society, personal needs, and lifestyle maintenance can take our eyes off of the word of God and focus on the world. Since many of us, like Peter, who was about to drown by looking at the high waves, are too busy being distracted by what's going on in our lives. We forget to focus on the giver of life. It takes discipline of various types of prayer *(especially praying in the spirit - or speaking in tongues),* studying the scriptures, staying connected to the body of Christ through fellowshipping and corporate worshiping, and learning how to stay in the secret place of the Most High - God the father. God will begin to illuminate your mind, and reveal what the world sees as mysteries that will never be a mystery to His sons and daughters. God wants to make Himself known to those whom He knows are truly His. Even while reading this book. Some of the most unbelievable events told here about my journey - will be well received by those who know the capacity of humankind to have encounters with demonically influenced people. People who unknowingly are hosts to destructive, life taking thieves called principalities, rulers of darkness and spiritual wickedness. Satan and his principalities have hated us from the time they were dismissed from heaven, cast out into outer darkness, until now. "The thief comes not but for to kill, steal, and destroy. I am come that they might have life, and that more abundantly." *(KJV. Bible. John 10:10)*

In retrospect

I have no regrets. It got scary, I'll have to admit. God wants to show us His glory, and we can't do it hiding in the closet at home. We can't say "God, please don't let it happen to me." We don't know what our life journey's will yield, or where it will take us. We just need to be aware that God's plans are to prosper us, and not to harm us; plans to give us hope and a bright future. For a long period of my life, I had suffered from low self esteem. This leads to self hatred and self condemnation and ultimately self rejection. I allowed the way others treated me, to dictate unrealistic negative things about my character. I felt like a nobody, always at entry level, always assisting, gophering, secondary; not realizing that I am "... a chosen generation, a royal priesthood, an holy nation, a peculiar people; that ye should shew forth the praises of him who hath called you out of darkness into his marvelous light:" *(I*

Peter 2:9) What a mandate! What a status! What a bright future! How could I be deceived by the lies of the devil to think any other way. What an honor and privilege to be trusted by my Heavenly Father, to endure the things I faced as a Christian in the marketplace and community. What were deemed destiny delays are now becoming turbo boosted to how God is blessing my life. I learned not to lean to my own limited understanding of things, as well as to trust in the Lord with all my heart. I'm so grateful to know that I don't have to control everything that happens in my life in order to be successful. I can call on the Holy Spirit, living inside of me, to lead and guide me into all truth. It's the most awesome feeling to have the living God occupying, dwelling in this body. It's even more awesome to learn how to decrease, so that God can increase Himself in me.

PRAYERS FOR YOU

Sound Mind

Father God, in the name of Jesus, I thank you that you have promised to give me power, love, and a sound mind. I thank you that I have the mind of Christ and hold the thoughts, feelings, and purposes of His heart. Father, I pray that you will help me to meditate only on your word and on positive things during this season of my life, and all the days of my life. I will meditate on things that are true and honest, just and pure, and lovely; things that are of a good report. I will meditate day and night on things that are virtuous and praiseworthy because you instructed me to do so through your word. I will constantly think about your words so that I can observe to do all that you command in it. Lord, you promised me that by doing this, I would make my way prosperous and that I would experience good success. Thank you for empowering me to be successful. Thank you for your promise to give me hope and a bright future. Thank you that the weapons will not prosper, that are formed against me. I will focus and keep my mind fixed on you, experiencing your amazing peace. I receive soundness of mind, and clarity in my thought processes. I receive your word and the leading of the Holy Spirit in everything that I do in Jesus's name I pray amen

Breaking the Spirit of Fear

Father God, in the name of Jesus, I break the spirit of fear off of my life. I command fear to loose me now. God has not given me a spirit of fear but of power, love, and a sound mind. Lord you said fear brings torment. I know that you promised me your peace if I focus on you. I receive your peace which surpasses understanding. Father, I thank you that your Supernatural peace will guard my heart and mind through Christ Jesus. Father God, I believe I receive your Supernatural peace. Your peace in me replaces fear now! I will not fear what man can do because you oh Lord are my helper. I saturate my mind, will, and emotions in the blood of Jesus. My heart will not fear, but will trust in you completely. I will not try to understand everything but I will always pray. I acknowledge you Lord in all my ways and you will make my path straight. Thank you for the power. Thank you for the love and thank you for the peace of mind in Jesus name, amen.

Indulgence in the Joy of the Lord

Father God, in the name of Jesus, I thank you that you give me strength when I rejoice in you. God I will laugh as you laugh at calamities. I will rejoice in you Lord always, for the joy of the Lord is my strength. I'm so grateful to you for all you've done for me, for your mercy, for your grace, for your goodness that follows me all the days of my life. I rejoice for your protection of me when I never knew I was in danger. I will laugh, for you said a merry heart does good like a medicine. I receive my healing today from the joy you give me. I receive my deliverance today. I rejoice in the God of my salvation, in Jesus' name, amen.

To Rest and Trust Fall on God

Father God you told me to trust in you with all my heart and not depend on my own understanding. You told me to acknowledge you in all my ways and you would direct my path. Lord, you said not to be wise in my own eyes but to reverence you and separate myself from evil which is doing it my way. You promised me that by doing this, I would be healed. As I trust in you Lord, I receive your peace to my soul. I will not focus on the enemies plans and schemes Lord, but I will trust and rest in you because you are my fortress. You are my refuge strength in times of trouble. I come praising you, thanking you, and worshiping you in your secret place and under the shadow of your wings, relaxing in you Lord. God, you protect me from all hurt, harm and danger. I throw my cares on you right now because you care for me. I will take on the burden of knowing who you are and how precious I am to you. You have loved me with an everlasting love. Lord, I exchange my heavy burdens for your peace. Abba, I appreciate the privilege of serving you and being called your son or daughter. Lord you told me to strive to enter into your rest, so I lay aside every weight and sin that throws me off the path. I will indulge in learning more of who you are and experience rest to my soul in Jesus is mighty name I pray, amen.

To Restore the fragmented soul

Lord you said that you are my shepherd and I have everything I need in you. I thank you for promising me protection, for leading me to a place of peace, and restoring my soul. I thank you for leading me in the path of righteousness for your namesake so that I am protected even at the face of death. Lord for every sin I've made that caused me to be at a place of frustration, I ask forgiveness. Anything in word, thought, or deed, that does not bring glory to your name in my life, I renounce it, I reject it, I resist it, and I rebuke it in the name of Jesus. I submit my mind, my will and my emotions to you Lord. You said If my people who are called by my name will humble themselves and pray, seek your face, and turn from our own way of doing things, you will then hear from heaven, forgive our sins, and heal our land. Father God, I seek your face right now and I ask you to baptize me afresh in your Spirit. Wash me in the blood of my Lord and Savior Jesus. I cover my mind, will, and emotions in the blood of Jesus, and I ask you to heal my soul. I speak healing into my life and restoration to my soul. I release the fire of God upon everything that brought damage into my life. I believe I receive my healing now in Jesus' name, amen.

About the Author

Yvette Eshiba is a locally known Minister of Yvette Eshiba Worship Ministries in the South Suburbs of Chicago. She hosts a podcast called 'Take It Back' and has multiple talents that include Voice Acting, Singing, Recording Artistry, and is an Educator, Community Leader, and Author. She is a single mother raising two beautiful children. Yvette is the sole proprietor of Eshiba Communications where she uses her voice to add vocal spice to businesses or authors who utilize audio books. She lives to learn and impact lives through personal experiences that will help others help themselves spiritually, mentally, and emotionally.

You can connect with me on:

f https://www.facebook.com/yvetteeshiba

Milton Keynes UK
Ingram Content Group UK Ltd.
UKHW030655120324
439302UK00015B/904